INSTANT EFL LE PLANS

25 CREATIVE, HIGHLY ENGAGING LESSON PLANS FROM PRACTICALLY NOTHING!

OTHER BOOKS BY ALPHABET PUBLISHING

60 *Positive Activities for Every Classroom*
Teresa X. Nguyen and Nathaniel Cayanan

60 *Positive Activities for Kids*
Teresa X. Nguyen and Tyler Hoang

Stories Without End: 24 *open-ended stories to engage students with reading,discussion, and creative writing*
Taylor Sapp

Successful Group Work: 13 *Activities to Teach Teamwork Skills*
Patrice Palmer

50 *Activities for the First Day of School*
Walton Burns

Classroom Community Builders: Activities for the First Day &
Beyond
Walton Burns

Keeping the Essence in Sight: From Teaching Practice to Reflection and Back Again
Sharon Hartle

We are a small, independent publishing company that specializes in creative resources for teachers in the area of English Language Arts and English as a Second or Other Language. We help stock the teacher toolkit with practical, useful, and innovative materials.

Sign up for our mailing list on our website, www.alphabetpublishingbooks.com, for teaching tips, updates on new books, and for discounts and giveaways you won't find anywhere else.

Instant EFL Lesson Plans

25 Creative, Highly Engaging Lesson Plans from Practically Nothing!

Cristian Spiteri

ISBN: 978-1-948492-34-8 (print)

        978-1-948492-84-3 (ebook)

Library of Congress Control Number: 2019935948

Alphabet Publishing
1204 Main St. #172
Branford, CT 06405
USA

info@alphabetpublishingbooks.com
www.alphabetpublishingbooks.com

Discounts on class sets and bulk orders available upon inquiry.

Cover by Bilsborough Designs

Interior Design by Red Panda Editorial Services.

Inspiration from LindseyAnne (https://www.youtube.com/watch?v=EN-r5amgXIF0) Flourishes by kio777 on Depositphotos. LumosLatino font by Franco Fernandez (http://fontmovie.blogspot.com/2015/11/font-lumus-latino.html). Other images licensed from DepositPhotos.

In the teaching profession, we often get ideas from our colleagues, training workshops, and even other books. The words in this book are the author's own, but he is indebted to others for some of the inspiration for the activities within. We have endeavored to give credit to the original sources. However, if you feel we have violated your rights or failed to acknowledge you, please do not hesitate to get in touch with us.

Country of Manufacture Specified on Last Page

First Printing 2019

Acknovlegdements

There are a couple of people whom I feel grateful to when I think back to my writing this book.

Special thanks go to Brandon Cachia, for helping me see the kind of teacher I could be and to Michael Bonnett, for believing in my book from the very first instant.

Thanks also go to my publisher, Walton Burns for being accommodating and enthusiastic with regards to my book.

CONTENTS

PREFACE

My aim with this book is to give you lesson plans you can use in a classroom with little to no preparation. The few that require resources only require them to be prepared once. Then you can keep them on hand to use again.

I wanted an instant tool that I could always take with me to class, without depending on the school to provide resources, printouts, and other materials. I hope these lesson plans will empower you the way they did me.

These lesson plans will engage and challenge your students, and they will also challenge you as the teacher. If you've taken the safe route until now, relying on student books in your lesson plans, using a lot of printouts, and not taking too many risks, then these lessons will stretch you beyond your comfort zone. As you become familiar with my framework, you will find yourself adapting and improving these lessons and even improvising more lessons. My director of studies observed my work and praised my lessons and methods. I'm confident that you will be praised too.

Obviously, you do not need to follow the lesson plans to the letter. Get comfortable with them, and adapt them as you see fit. However, I encourage you not to skip any bits just because you're afraid it's silly or you're afraid your students won't cooperate or you're just too embarrassed to do it. Those lesson plans will be of greatest benefit to you and a great learning opportunity for your students. If some activities are particularly uncomfortable for you, then try to apply them when you are teaching a class that you feel comfortable with and close to. That way, it won't be as hard.

Some of these activities are complex, so a part of successful implementation is asking instruction-checking and concept-checking questions to your students to make sure that they understand what is expected of them. In fact, any time you give your students rules, I recommend you ask them to repeat the rules back to you, as well.

Don't be surprised if you find yourself being liked more by some of your students. Don't be discouraged if you start being liked less by others. Unfortunately, not everyone is aware that learning *can* be fun. Some students believe that if they are having fun, they can't possibly be learning, and so they give negative feedback. Ignore it; these lessons all follow TEFL methodologies and have clear objectives.

CIRCLE OF LIFE

LEVEL: *any.*

AIMS: *Students will get to know the teacher better. The teacher will be humanized.*

RESOURCES: *Whiteboard. It will be of use to you if you can memorize or write down a list of words to write in your circle to have on hand every time you do this activity.*

I RECOMMEND DOING this lesson when you're just starting to get to know a group, such as on the first day.

Ensure your students know your name, and draw a huge circle on the board. Label this circle "Teacher's Circle of Life," replacing *teacher* with your name. Inside the circle, write a list of stuff that is important and meaningful to you—but without details, just a name or a word. Go ahead and populate your circle. Once you have, explain to your students that you've written down a bunch of very important things about yourself in the circle, but that you would like them to guess the significance of these terms you've put down.

For inspiration, in case you're feeling blocked, here is a list of the terms I like to use:

- My hometown
- Sophie—my cat
- Sookie—my dog
- 10—my shoe size
- Wicked—my favorite Broadway show
- Athens—my last holiday
- Tuscany—my next trip
- Joseph—my best friend
- UOM—where I got my education
- 8—the month I was born (after they guess this, I often ask them to guess my star sign)
- My favorite artist

Let the students put their hands up, and when you call on them, listen to their guess as to what one of the terms in the circle signifies for you. Feel free to let some of your humor show here, if you're comfortable.

I suggest that you not give away the answer. Instead just give clues, giving away the answer only if the class is completely unresponsive or too shy. For example, I like to tell my students an anecdote: In my household, we have a rule that every pet we adopt has to have a name that starts with S. After I tell the anecdote, I ask my students, "So who do you think Sophie is?" This applies here as well as anywhere else. I never give away my answers freely.

If you have a shy group, you might find yourself presenting them the Circle of Life, explaining the process, and being faced with a class of students who just stare at you. Don't panic. As teachers we can feel like something is wrong or we are not doing enough when the classroom falls to silence. But try to stick with it; give the students some time to contribute answers. If, in two minutes, the students' faces are still blank, then start calling on them one by one and asking them to contribute a guess. Not all students are used to classroom environments where the students are expected to speak.

Sometimes, after the Circle of Life is completed, some students may be willing to contribute their own circle and carry out the same activity. If this happens, feel free to let them, time-permitting.

An interesting alternative, if you become bored of the Circle of Life, is to draw a timeline and mark some important dates in your life without marking why they are important. Students then have the opportunity to ask some questions to get clues and guess why each date is important to you.

I learned about this activity during TEFL training at E.F. Malta. It was first published by Alan Marsh on onestopenglish.com.

WHAT A FUNNY NAME

LEVEL: *any*.

AIMS: *Students will get the opportunity to speak in front of the class and become more engaged. Students will get to know each other's names. Students will practice their sense of humor.*

RESOURCES: *Whiteboard and markers. It will also be of use to you if you can memorize a funny anecdote about your name.*

THIS ACTIVITY IS meant to be used as an introduction and works well on the first day of class.

Write out your name in large capital letters across the board. Then tell your students a funny anecdote, which may or may not be true, about your name. I tell my students that I was named after an Italian actor, because he was known to be the most beautiful actor in the world, and I tell them that my life has been a constant struggle with all the people who spell my name wrong, insisting that they put an *h* where they shouldn't.

I then tell my students that there are some markers waiting for them on the desk. One by one, in any order they want, they should go to the board, grab a marker, and write out their name, making it somehow link to one of the names already on the board, as in a crossword puzzle shape (for example, if the name on the board is CRISTIAN and the student is writing the name MARIA, she must make either the I or the A link to the corresponding letter in my name). Then they should tell an interesting or funny story about their name.

Explain that the story does not need to be true; this is just for fun. If there is no possible position where a student can link their name to the names on the board, they can just write their name on any space they want on the board. I recommend doing this exercise with students who are shy and look like they will have a hard time speaking throughout their lessons.

FOUR TRUTHS, ONE LIE

LEVEL: *Best with students who are at least A2 (pre-intermediate) level.*

AIMS: *Students will be engaged. Familiarity, warmth, and humor will be introduced inside the classroom. The students will get to know each other better.*

RESOURCES: *None.*

THIS LESSON IS ideal in a multinational classroom.

Ask for a volunteer. If no one comes forward within a minute, choose someone yourself. Ask them to leave the room and sit somewhere out of earshot.

Then speak to the rest of the class and instruct them that they need to come up with five questions to ask the volunteer, who will henceforth be referred to as the *prisoner*. The questions should be personal, not factual.

For example, "What is the weather like today?" is not good. "What's your favorite weather like?" is better.

The prisoner is invited to return and stand or sit the center of the room, then is instructed to answer five questions from classmates. However, the prisoner must answer four questions truthfully and one question with a lie. The prisoner should try their best to bluff, because afterward, the classmates will have to guess the lie.

Once the prisoner has answered the five questions, they are instructed to wait outside once more. Tell the class that they have one or two minutes to decide which of the prisoner's answers was the lie.

The prisoner is then invited back into the classroom and confronted with the accusation as to which of their answers was the lie. At this point they can tell the class if they were right or wrong.

You can reuse the process a couple more times, if the students are getting into it. And if the students are volunteering themselves to be the prisoner, that's a great sign.

FOLLOW THE LEADER

LEVEL: *any*

AIMS: *Students will be engaged. Familiarity, warmth, and humor are will be introduced inside the classroom. Students will be forced to get out of their comfort zone and slowly start being more at ease in the classroom.*

RESOURCES: *None, but for the dancing part of this lesson, it is a good idea to have some source of music, like a student's phone.*

THIS IS GOOD for a first day activity.

Ask for a volunteer or select a contestant. Have the contestant leave the room and wait somewhere out of earshot.

Ask for a volunteer dance leader and a volunteer DJ to play music on their phone.

At this point, you're likely to experience a great deal of resistance. Many students will be deflecting the leader role. Tell your students that they have two minutes to pick out the leader and DJ before the contestant returns.

If the students are still struggling to pick the leader after the two minutes, then it will be up to you to select students for the roles. Do not choose a student that looks very anxious, as such a student might need to be eased into the classroom before they will be comfortable with such a role.Remember that many students are used to a classroom where a teacher speaks and they just sit there—and asking them to do something or be the center of attention might trigger panic in them. It doesn't mean that the activity should be skipped. It actually makes it even more important, but we need to give time and patience to the students so they can open up.

Explain that the students need to stand in a circle and pretend they are in a club, dancing. The leader will dance, while everyone else in the circle has to echo the leader's movements and routines. The DJ will be in charge of putting on music (using their phone or MP3 player or class CD player).

Leader elected, music on? Okay. Have the group form their circle and dance following the leader's moves while trying to keep the identity of the leader inconspicuous. For example, they shouldn't look at the leader constantly. Invite the contestant back to the center of the classroom and have them count to ten before opening their eyes. This gives the others time to form their circle around the contestant. The group starts dancing and playing music, and the contestant tries to guess the identity of the leader. When the contestant has guessed correctly, the round is over. You can give a limited number of guesses if you wish.

After the round is over, you can repeat a couple of times with different contestants, leaders, and DJs.

THIS IS ME—POSTER / ENVELOPE EDITION

LEVEL: *any, but works best with A2 (pre-intermediate) and above.*

AIMS: *Students will be engaged in the activity, and have a chance to get to know each other more. Students will talk about their passions, hobbies, and experiences, while bonding with the other students.*

RESOURCES: *All the participants will need a sheet of paper and a pen or pencil. Just in case, I always carry a pile of paper I can give to my students.*

If you're going for the envelope edition, you can supply your students with medium-sized or large envelopes instead of a sheet of paper. Don't go for small envelopes; go for medium or large ones. You will also need blue tack—but you would only need to acquire this once, and then reuse it for every time you carry out this session with a different group.

THIS LESSON WILL work amazingly in a multilingual class. I recommend the envelope edition if the class is going to be staying for longer than a week. It will really give the opportunity to nurture friendships. This is interesting if done as the last thing on the first day.

Make sure your students understand the terms *passion* and *passionate*—pre-teach them, or use hangman and then explain. The less you give the explanation away for free, the better, as usual. *Passion* may be close to the students' native language, so they might surprise you.

Explain to the students that they all have a sheet of paper (or envelope) and on it they must write their names in large lettering. Their next task is to draw on the paper all the things that make up who they are, their hobbies, interests, passions, and anything else that they feel represents them. No writing is allowed, only drawing. It's not an issue if the students are terrible at drawing; it probably makes the next part more fun.

As your students are preparing the poster, you (the teacher) should prepare one for yourself—of course this applies only the first time you do this activity. After that, you should get your paper laminated or stored in a plastic folder, so you can reuse it as needed. After everyone is done with their drawings (set a time limit—no more than ten minutes), let the students reveal and hold up their drawings.

After that, set up the posters all around the room, on desks and places where they are easily seen. Explain the process to the students: What they have to do is go around the room and look at other people's posters, taking this opportunity to get to know each other. They can ask questions about what a drawing means and then other questions about that topic, so if a student drew a cat, someone could ask them "How many cats do you have?" and "How old are they?"

At first, you might need to illustrate with examples. The chatty ones will follow suit, with an exchange of information and familiarity going on through the classroom. Let this activity come to a natural end, don't rush it.

If you went for the envelope edition, then give each student a small piece of blue tack, and instruct them to attach their envelope with all their drawings somewhere around the room. Afterward, tell them that they can make use of those envelopes, to deliver gifts, letters, and secret notes to each other.

FIND SOMEONE WHO?

LEVEL: *A2 (pre-intermediate) and above. You can do this with A1 (beginner), but I recommend that you choose the phrases according to the level. For example, a present perfect phrase should only be used with classrooms that are at least at the B1 (intermediate) level.*

AIMS: *Students will be engaged and will interact with each other. Students will study or review the verb tenses.*

RESOURCES: *All the participants will need a sheet of paper and a pen or pencil. Just in case, I always carry a pile of paper I can give to my students. The lesson needs a list of phrases for the Find Someone Who game. I recommend that you print a list once (see the example in this book) and laminate it or put it in a folder (it can be the other side of the poster sheet) and attach it to the board. If you're in a pinch and did not have time to prepare the list, just copy the phrases for the Find Someone Who game to the board.*

THIS IS AN excellent early lesson plan to revise verb tenses or introduce a new one.

Let your students see the "find someone who" phrases, and instruct them to copy them onto their paper. After that, assign the students to look at each phrase, determine its grammatical tense (simple present, etc.), and then change the phrase into a question with the same tense. Have them work on this on their own or in pairs according to their level (lower levels should work in pairs).

After that, tell the class that you will go through the phrases together. As you go, have students correct each other's mistakes, and also get them to explain the meaning and reason for the tenses and sentences, e.g., "Why are we using the present continuous here?" to get them to say that the present continuous can be used for the future.

If you feel like it's needed, this is a good time to get into the different grammatical tenses. Go through the tenses that were challenging and draw up, in cooperation with your students, a thorough table for how to work out these tenses (including negative statements and questions) and what their uses are. It's ideal to point out the distinctions between some tenses that have similar uses, or are worded and worked out similarly. If you need any grammatical notes going into this, you can use google or even a phone app. If you suspect your students might be able to handle the task, make *them* be the ones to draw out the tense and its uses on the board, with you doing error correction at the end. Your students might pleasantly surprise you. Ensure that the difference between present perfect and simple past is made clear and that the students understand that present continuous can be used to talk about the future.

When the grammar lesson is over, explain the rules of the game. The students must go around speaking to everyone in the class and ask them the questions that they've conjured for the phrases in the Find Someone Who game. When they get an affirmative answer, instruct them that they must write the name of the person next to the phrase, but encourage them to also use this opportunity to get to know the other person better. You can illustrate this with an example:

"Have you been to Rome?"
"Yes."
"Great, Rome is one of my favorite cities. What did you like best about Rome?"
"The Coliseum" or "Pizza," etc.
"Who did you go with?"
And so on. At the end explain to them that you will ask them to share with you the most interesting things they learned about each other.

Let the activity take as long as it needs, then get feedback. You can even ask the students who they found out they have something in common with and use this opportunity to teach them the phrase "in common."

FIND SOMEONE WHO...

Find Someone Who ...	Names
has read more than 10 books	
has been to Asia	
doesn't use Facebook	
took a selfie today	
rarely eats fish	
enjoys sports	
is an only child	
has 2 or more pets	
has 3 syllables in their name	
has over one hundred followers on Instagram	
is scared to watch horror films alone	
plays an instrument	
has a favorite video game	
has the same eye color as you	
has tried Italian food	

PHOTOCOPIABLE

How Long Does It Take to Get There?

LEVEL: *I recommend A2 to B1 (pre-intermediate to interme-diate), although I've used this lesson successfully with A1 (beginner) students, but they were exceptionally good students. This could work with B2 (upper-intermediate) if there is a need for geographic understanding, but be prepared to make it more challenging.*

AIMS: *Students will be engaged. Students will revise grammat-ical tenses as well as lexis relating to travel and to time taken to arrive somewhere. Students will be introduced to geography and talk about their travels and experiences.*

RESOURCES: *A map of the geographic location of the school. Time-permitting, you can prepare a printed, maybe laminated, map. For example, I teach English in Maltese schools and am familiar with the geography, so I have a map of the Maltese Islands. If you don't have a printed map, you can find one on your phone.*

THIS LESSON EARNED me tremendous praise from my director of studies, and I wholeheartedly recommend it.

Ask for a volunteer to be your artist, or select one. Give this student a map of your area. Have the artist draw the outline of the map on the board, taking up a great deal of space, even half the board. As the artist is drawing, ask the rest of the class if they know what the artist is drawing.

Once the drawing is complete the map can slowly start to be filled in. Together, identify major features, areas, or cities. As always, let your students try to give you the answers. If, during the **Circle of Life** game, you shared your hometown, ask your students if they remember it; surprisingly, they always do.

Ask them to guess the location of your hometown on the map. Then mark it. Ask them about the location of the school, the name of the city. When they have it, ask them to point it out on the map, and mark it.

Then ask them what you do every morning. They will come up with myriad answers, but the one you are waiting for is that you go to work.Ask them, "How do I get to work?" and wait for them to give the correct answer, such as "You drive to work," "You take the bus," or "by bike."

Ask them, "How long does it take me to get here?" Invite various students to come up with some guesses, and then finally give the correct answer. Write a sentence on the board, such as "It takes me about 30 minutes to get to work from home by car."

Drill this with your students. By *drill* I mean say a word or phrase with the correct pronunciation and intonation and have the students repeat it. Also ask them about the use of *about* and what it means (that is, that it's not exactly 30 minutes, but varies slightly from day to day.)

Next, ask them to tell you where they are staying. They may tell you the city where their hotel or host family is located. Ask them to indicate it on the map on the board. (It is ideal that the map drawn up at the beginning of the lesson should include students' likely accommodation areas in its scope.)

Ask them to write down a sentence about their trip every day from their accommodation to school, modeled after your example sentence. Assign a time limit, say two minutes. Invite one student to write their sentence on the board. Perform error correction.

Importantly, ask them to identify the tense of the two sentences on the board (simple present) and ask them why they are using the simple present. The correct answer is that the journey or action is repeated every day. Instruct the students to write the sentences down.

Change the focus again. Tell your students about something you did recently, like the day before or the previous weekend. Tell them that you went to get a haircut or went to see your best friend.

Ask if they can remember your best friend's name from the **Circle of Life** game. Tell them where your best friend lives (or where the hair salon is) and ask them to guess its location on the map. Then ask them how they think you got there (on foot, by car?) and how long the trip took. After giving your true answers, put that sentence on the board.

For example, "Yesterday evening I went to meet my friend. It took me 12 minutes by car to get to her house from home." You might ask, "Do I need to add *about* here?" If they say no, ask why, and the correct answer should be that this happened in the past and you know exactly how long it took you.

At this point, instruct the students to write down their own sentences about what they did yesterday (or some other recent date). After three minutes, select one student to write their sentence on the board, and perform error correction.

Ask them what tense the sentences are in (simple past) and ask them why (because the action happened at a defined time in the past). Ask the students to copy the sentences (yours and their peer's corrected sentence) on paper.

Wipe off the sentences, and then tell the students about a plan of yours for the near future, such as that night or the following day. Identify the location on the map, and ask them to guess how long the trip is and how you're getting there.

After giving your answer, write the sentences on the board, for example, "This weekend I am meeting my friend at the department store to buy clothes. I am going by car, and it should take me 30 minutes to get there." Ask the students why we use *should*. The correct answer is because you don't know exactly yet how much time it will take, but based on past experience, you assume that 30 minutes is accurate.

Then ask the students to write their own sentences about some plan they have for the future. Select one student to write on the board, and then perform error correction. Ask them about what tense was used and why. Essentially, more than one tense is correct here, and it's important that the students understand that we can use the present continuous, *be + going to*, or *will* to talk about the future.

Take this opportunity to talk about something that is geographically and culturally relevant to your area, to expand the students' knowledge. In my case, on Malta, I'll tell them about a trip I took to Gozo to attend the carnival. I will ask them,

"How did I get to Gozo?"
"By ferry"
"But how did I get on the ferry? Did I just get up and go on the ferry?"
"No, you drove your car to the port"
"And at the port what did I do with my car?"
"You drove it onto the ferry and took it with you to Gozo."
And then I show them the location on the map where I arrive, Nadur, to attend Carnival festivities. While I go through this I check in with them and ask how long each part of the trip took me. If your students are struggling, keep guiding them and helping them to figure out the process.

After this exercise, ask the students to write down sentences about your trip, detailing each part, and saying how long your journey was. Allow them up to 20 minutes so they have time to write down the trip in detail, and answer any questions they come up with while they're writing, like "Where did you stay?" or "What time did you leave your home?," etc.

When they're done with the writing, select a student to write their sentences on the board. Perform error correction, double-checking the understanding of the use of the grammatical tense. Then tell the students to copy the sentences down.

Next ask the artist you selected to draw the map of a place related to the students—their hometown, or their country if they are all from the same location, or a map of the countries where they live. You can select multiple students if more than one country will be needed.

Invite the students to come to the board to talk about where they live, where their school is, where their home is, how they spend their free time and where they go. Ask them questions like "How do you get there?" and "Is it easier, cheaper, faster to get there by bus or by train?"

Ask them to tell you about their holidays and their trips, where they spend them, with whom, and how they get there. They may talk about airplanes or ferries they needed to catch, the Chunnel, or other means they used for their trips. Then ask them to describe their trips and talk about where they stayed, what they liked, and what they did. Feel free to ask for more information: I once mentioned briefly during this activity that I was going to Tuscany the following month, when one of the students insisted on coming to the board to show me the region of Tuscany on the map and tell me about his favorite cities and towns in the region.

HEROES

LEVEL: *I recommend B1 (intermediate) and up. You can make this lesson more challenging by choosing even more difficult occupational vocabulary.*

AIMS: *Students will be engaged, Students will learn new vocabulary related to careers and job titles. Students will participate in a debate. Students will build soft skills and ability to work and share their opinion in pairs and groups.*

RESOURCES: *None, but students will need a piece of paper and a pen. I recommend having access to some scratch paper you can give to students, for the occasional students who have yet to realize that they should always bring writing material to class.*

THIS LESSON WAS adapted from *Teen World* by Joanna Budden, Cambridge University Press. 2009.

Introduce the term *heroes* to the students—I use a game of hangman.

Tell the students that they're going to participate in a live focus group, or survey, and draw a horizontal line across the board.

On this line, mark five points, evenly spaced, and label each one. Get your students to try to guess what term you're going to put next to each point, with the correct answers being "Strongly agree," "Somewhat agree," "Neutral," "Somewhat disagree," and "Strongly disagree."

Tell the students that you are going to read a sentence aloud and that the students have to identify how they feel in relation to the sentence you just read.

Once they've identified whether they agree, disagree, or stand somewhere in between, they are to stand in a line in front of the phrase on the board that matches their feelings.

Say the following sentences out loud:

"Heroes exist only in comics and movies."
"I have my own hero in my life."
"I think I am a hero sometimes."
Stop between sentences to ask students to share their opinions before reading the next sentence.

Once students are back in their seats, assign each of them a job in secret, writing it for them on a piece of paper.

Teacher	Nurse	Life coach
Firefighter	Surgeon	Lifeguard
Police officer	Psychologist	Medical researcher
Soldier	Farmer	Social worker
Aid worker	Politician	Environmental lawyer
Self-made millionaire	Environmental activist	

Pre-teach the more challenging vocabulary. Also, feel free to go against gender stereotypes, so pick a female millionaire, a male nurse, etc. I recommend assigning politician to a particularly confident student, as that student can have a harder job than the others in the next part of the task, when they will have to convince others why they deserve to be called heroes.

Tell the students that they are going to have ten minutes to prepare an identity around this career that they were assigned. They can decide a name, age, and other life details, but most importantly, they need to see themselves as heroes in their job, and it's their task to come up with why they are heroic in their position. Urge them to think about great things they have achieved or people they've saved, or other accomplishments to make the world a better place. Examples can include a millionaire who invests money into a charity to help campaign for equality, or a teacher who opened a school for poor kids in Africa, or a police officer who caught a terrorist.

When they're done, tell them to imagine they're attending a mixer, where all sorts of heroic people have been invited, and it's their job to attend this mixer, meet the other participants, and convince everybody of their heroicness. Inform the students to carry a piece of paper so that as they go, they can write down the name and the job of every person they meet. Let the activity take as long as it needs; until the students have met every other person and written down their name and job.

When your students are back in their seats, select an artist, and ask the artist to draw a desert island on the board. Let the class have fun with this; let them draw trees, monkeys, or whatever else. Tell them that the island is surrounded by sharks.

Tell them that the heroes that were at the party decided to go on a trip, but the plane crashed, and the heroes all ended up stranded on the desert island. After an inspection of the island, it was determined that it only contained enough food to feed five people. Instruct your students to work alone, focus on their paper, and think about who the five people who survive should be. Give them two minutes. Instruct them to work alone.

When this is done, instruct students that they are going to work in pairs with the person sitting next to them. In these pairs, students have to discuss their opinions about who they decided to kill and let live, and then the two of them have to come to a mutual decision about the five survivors. Assign a five-minute time limit.

In the next step, combine each pair with another, to make groups of four. Instruct your students to work in these groups and repeat the process to come to a unanimous decision. Give them five to seven minutes.

Instruct your students to form a circle with their chairs. Explain that they will have to debate together and finally choose the five survivors. Select a chairperson for the group who will be responsible for making sure that everyone gets to give their opinion and that everybody speaks English, and aggregating everybody's opinions and presenting the five survivors to you. Assign a 15-20-minute time limit, but if the debate is still going strong, feel free to let it run longer. At the end, ask the chairperson to tell you who the five survivors are.

If you want to lengthen this lesson, you can improvise additional scenarios, especially if the class is enjoying the lesson. You can tell them, while having an artist draw, that a kraken has emerged from the seas and has asked them for a human sacrifice in exchange for not killing all of them, and make them debate who the sacrifice should be. Another example is to imagine a shipwreck nearby. A survivor turns up on the island, and the students debate what to do with this survivor.

WHERE WAS THIS?

LEVEL: *A2–B2 (pre-intermediate to upper-intermediate), can be used with A1 (beginner) with some scaffolding.*

AIMS: *Students will be engaged. Students will practice their prepositions in a humorous, fun setting.*

RESOURCES: *This task relies on describing the position of objects that have been moved around the room. Hence, this lesson goes well after a prepositions lesson or worksheet, but that is not mandatory. This task in itself does not require any resources beyond normal classroom items.*

Ask for two or three volunteers. Once you have your volunteers, ask them to take a good look around the classroom, observing and noticing everything they can.

Ask the volunteers to leave the classroom and go somewhere out of earshot. Ask the remaining students to change three things in the classroom. They can move stuff around, turn lights on or off, open or close windows or shutters, or whatever they come up with.

Invite the volunteers back in and ask them to identify what has changed. Let them know that just pointing at what has changed will not be enough; they will need to verbally tell you.

Ask another group to try the same exercise, until all those who want to try it have gotten a turn.

You can turn this into a competition or a timed exercise to make it more exciting.

MOST INSPIRING HUMAN

LEVEL: *B2 (upper intermediate) and up.*

AIMS: *Students will be encouraged to use their imagination. Students will be encouraged to improvise and speak in front of a class, engaging their public speaking skills and their confidence.*

RESOURCES: *None.*

If your class's energy level seems too low, or they feel overly shy, then an energizer like **Follow the Leader** might be a good intro to this activity.

A body warm-up or voice warm-up from YouTube might also entertain your students and be helpful. I sometimes use some neck exercises and simple yoga poses; and for the voice, I ask my students to speak with a (clean) pen in their mouth in pairs (lying horizontally between their top and bottom teeth). The reaction is usually giggles, but I tell them that this exercise warms up their voices and makes them less likely to get tongue-tied. I ask them also to pair up and stand two meters away from their peer, then carry out conversations at that distance without anyone leaning forward. This helps with students who are shy speaking in a foreign language and as a result speak too softly.

Encourage your students to relax for this lesson. Tell them that they are leaving their lives behind and instead imagining wholly different new ones where they can be, achieve, or do whatever they dream. Encourage them to dream big and think about their careers. If they could have any job or career in the world, what would they be doing? Assign a few minutes for brainstorming. Then, ask your students for their ideas. Expect things like millionaires, entrepreneurs, authors, astronauts, artists, actors, singers, philanthropists, fashion magazine editors, star athletes, etc.

Select half the students that had the more interesting ideas (with no overlap, so everyone should have a unique idea). Have those students sit in one part of the classroom, and tell them that their job is to completely immerse themselves in imagining a different life where they successfully achieved their dreams. Encourage them to go into minute details, things like whether they're married or have kids, how they built their success, what steps they took, whether they've donated to charities or made some contributions to society.

Instruct the other half of the students that they are going to be attending an event called Most Inspiring Human 2019 (or whatever year it is) and they will hear speeches by some people who have built great careers. They are going to be reporters, asking these people questions about their lives. Help build some fluency at this point by helping them build questions that a famous or successful person is likely to be asked. "What was it like working with [insert name of famous person] on this project?" "What would you say to young people who wish to follow in your footsteps?" "What makes you unique?" and so on. Assign 20 minutes for this brainstorming activity. Explain to the reporters that they also have the task of judging and awarding one of the speakers the Most Inspiring 2019 award.

After 20 minutes of brainstorming, during which you can hover and help out some students, start inviting students one by one to come to the front of the classroom to share their story and at the end answer questions from the reporters. Let each speaker have around ten minutes, more if it's going well. When all the speakers are done, let the reporters discuss in a group who will win the award. You can make a fake celebration and have your reporters improvise a trophy that they will present to the winner, along with cheers and applause.

AT THE RESTAURANT

LEVEL: *A2 (pre-intermediate) and up.*

AIMS: *Students will be made to improvise, building their confidence in speaking in a second language without having too much time to think. Students will have fun talking about food, working on menus from different cuisines, and learning terms related to personality.*

RESOURCES: *Paper role cards (see the next page). I recommend you print them and cut them once, so that you never need to prepare them again; laminate them if possible. If you absolutely cannot get your hands on these, then just write them up quickly on some pieces of paper (maybe in fewer words or even just one word) while the students are brainstorming, and then cut them up. You will also need some blank sheets of paper for the students to make menus; but if you cannot get any, then you can skip the menus.*

Introduce the topic of restaurants in any way you like to your students. Tell them that you want them to help you remember the categories of dishes you can have at a restaurant (starter, main course, side dish, dessert, beverages), and write them on the board as you go. Put your students in groups, and give them five minutes to come up with all the dishes they can for each category (some overlap is normal).

Choose some students to write their dishes on the board for a particular category. Instruct the students to check their classmates' work for any mistakes, and suggest more dishes if they know any. At this point you may elicit more dishes from your students through questions. You may also teach other related language like *tips*, *the bill*, and *chef*.

Put students in teams of four to six members. Get each team to choose a specific type of restaurant (Chinese, Japanese, Indian, Italian...). Then, instruct each team to work together to write up a menu for that restaurant, making it as complete as they can. Allow them to use the internet on their phones, as they will probably need to. Assign a maximum of ten minutes.

Tell the students that they are going to role-play being in a restaurant and that you are going to give each of them a role card with a personality (or adjective if you didn't have time to prepare the role cards). One person in each team will have to be the server (If the teams are too small, choose a server from the opposing team). Instruct the students that, in their teams they are going to improvise and role-play going to a restaurant together as a group of friends, bringing with them this new personality. Give them a few minutes to prepare (not more than five, ideally much less), and then ask them to start performing (explain or elicit the meaning of improv or improvisation if the students don't know it). Tell the students that each team's performance needs to be ten minutes long, and you will let them know when only one minute remains.

If the students are struggling during the performance, help them out by asking questions such as "What happens next?" or "Where are you now?" or "Do you see or smell anything strange?"

If you have already done Mask Work with your students, then a variation on this lesson plan could be done wearing the masks during the restaurant role-play instead of role cards. Students would have to improvise how their mask-character would behave in this restaurant.

RESTAURANT ROLE CARDS

A. You have never been to a restaurant like this before, so you don't know what a fork or knife is, what the menu is, and what any of the dishes are. You constantly ask questions because you don't understand anything, and you're very annoying.

B. You love this restaurant, and you visit it very often. You're annoyingly cheerful and you know all the food on the menu, because you've tried everything. You keep telling everybody how amazing this restaurant is, and how almost all the dishes are your favorite dish. You order loads of everything.

C. You are a health nut. You've seen a video on the internet about MSG/Gluten/etc., and are concerned about all the food at the restaurant and if it's actually healthy. You ask too many questions to the waiter/waitress about the contents of the food, and keep annoying your friends telling them about how bad MSG can be for their health.

D. You don't have much money, and you don't want to spend it at the restaurant. Keep complaining that everything is too expensive, or try suggesting a cheaper restaurant. Don't order any wine or drinks except water. Tell people about how much cheaper it would be to make the same dish at home.

E. You like showing off. You tell people about all the amazing places you've travelled to, all the famous people you've dined with, and all the expensive, amazing restaurants you've eaten at. You keep telling your friends that this restaurant is OK, but not too impressive, because you are used to expensive restaurants and places.

F. You complain a lot. Everything in this restaurant is a problem for you. The chairs, the food, the service, the weather, the temperature. You eat, but you hate the food.

PHOTOCOPIABLE

WHAT DO YOU LOOK FOR IN A LIFE PARTNER?

LEVEL: *B1 (intermediate) and up.*

AIMS: *Students will be made to improvise. Students will learn higher-level lexis items like deal-breakers and subtlety. Students will talk about dating in a humorous manner, and be given the opportunity to get creative deciding how to approach the dating scene.*

RESOURCES: *None, although students might need some paper to write on. It's best to keep a stack of scratch paper handy.*

Elicit the term *speed dating* (maybe through hangman) and then elicit its meaning. Then present the question "What do you look for in a life partner?" and ask them what this means to them. List responses in one column on the board, and then leave another column blank.

Elicit from them the term *deal breakers*, and ask them what it means (something you will absolutely not put up with). Write "deal break-ers" as the title of the second column.

Tell your students to imagine that they are going to attend a speed dating event in the near future, and they need to think ahead and write down what things they look for in a life partner, as well as their deal-breakers.

During the process, elicit and teach terms that are related to this activity. In particular, elicit all the different phrases and terms we can use to say that someone is attractive, and ask the students to help you distinguish which we can use with males and which we can use with females.

Get some feedback and ideas from the students (for both categories), and write them on the board, taking the opportunity to teach any difficult terms or correct a few errors.

Ask them how they would find out if the person they're on a date with meets the criteria they want. If they said that they want someone who's rich or intelligent, ask them how they would find that out about the person in front of them. Ask them, "Would you ask that person?" and see their reaction. When they say that they wouldn't just ask, ask them why, and get them to say that it's rude or impolite.

Ask them what they are going to do then, if they want to find out about their date. Elicit from them that they would ask something that isn't rude and direct, but gives you an indication regarding what you want—questions like "What school did you go to?" "What work do you do?" "Where do you live?" "How many languages do you speak?" or "Where did you last go on holiday?"

When your students understand the concept of asking discreetly for what they want to know, so as not to offend, teach them that we call this *being subtle*. Drill the pronunciation of *subtle*, and get them to tell you that the *b* is silent.

Commence the speed dating event: split the class in two, put half on one side, forming a line with their chair, and the other half forming a line across from them, so candidates are sitting opposite each other.

Tell the students that they are at a speed dating event and are going to see if any of the candidates are the right partner for them while trying to be subtle. Tell them that when you clap, the students on the outer line will all move one step to the right so they can meet a new partner. Keep clapping until each student has spoken to every person in the opposite line, and clap every three minutes.

At the end you can take some feedback and even ask some students if they think they found any matches.

LANGUAGE AND THE BODY

LEVEL: *A2 (pre-intermediate) and up, although the harder part of this activity is better suited for B1 (intermediate) and up.*

AIMS: *Students' knowledge of the body will be activated in a fun manner, as well as their knowledge of expressions related to the body. Students will get the opportunity to share and learn about other languages and the way other languages use the body in everyday speech.*

RESOURCES: *None*

Divide students into two groups (ideally mixing nationalities as much as possible), and tell them that you need one volunteer. Explain that you are going to show a word to the volunteer, who will try to reveal it to the groups but without speaking, only miming and gesturing. Concept-check, to make sure students understand the instructions.

Start the game of charades using body words. Keep the same volunteers throughout the activity. Pick words that are gradually more challenging, and instruct your teams that when they guess the word, they don't need to say anything, but they need to write it down. If your volunteers prefer pointing to indicate the body part, allow it. Tell the teams that accurate spelling is important. If you need words, use the following:

Arms	Eyebrow	Leg
Cheekbones	Eyes	Neck
Chest	Foot	Nostril
Chin	Forehead	Scalp
Collarbone	Hands	Shoulders
Ears	Knee	Throat

After the volunteers have acted out all the words, instruct the volunteer to check each group's list and correct them. Let the volunteer check which team has the most correct (and correctly spelled) answers and is the winner.

Let one of the volunteers take the reins of the classroom for a while. Let the volunteer have the list. Instruct them to do error correction with the class, finding the problem words, double-checking the meaning with the class, and correcting any spelling mistakes. Only interfere if the volunteer tries to teach pronunciation wrong, as you don't want your students to learn the wrong pronunciation, but keep your attitude more laid-back, showing your volunteer that you trust them to do a good job. Congratulate your volunteer on a good job leading the classroom and keeping an eye out for mistakes. It helps build confidence.

If students have not pointed this out yet, elicit from them that the theme of the charades game was the body. Let the volunteer return to their group, and then present on the board a list of expressions that use parts of the body. Tell the students that they have 10 to 15 minutes to discuss them in groups and figure out their meaning. If you need a list of expressions, use the list in the first column below.

Expression	Meaning
Absence makes the heart grow fonder	You miss someone more when they are away
Lend a hand	Help someone out
The gift of gab	Be really good at speaking
Cost an arm and a leg	Very expensive
Have a green thumb	Good at gardening
Break a leg	Good luck (used in theater)
Pull someone's leg	Play a trick on someone
Wear your heart on your sleeve	Be honest about your feelings
Head over heels	Fall in love
Look a gift horse in the mouth	Fail to appreciate a good thing

After the students have looked at the expressions for a few minutes, write again, on another side of the board, the answers in the second column of the table, but in random order. Explain to your students that they have to match the expressions with their respective meanings.

When the students' time is up, have them combine into a single group and together agree to a single answer for the meaning of each expression. This is powerful, especially in a multinational class, as the students will be making associations with their L1s and trying to explain how they came to the conclusion and why they think their answer is the right one. Have them present their answers, and do error correction.

Let the students return to their group, and tell them to think of body expressions they know that come from their L1s and other languages that they speak besides English. Give them a few minutes to do this. When they are done, invite some students, one by one, to come to the front of the classroom and write down their expression on the board, and then either explain the meaning to the class or quiz the class to see if anyone gets it.

Lastly, explain to the group that in the English language, we tend to equate personality traits with the heart. Use expressions like *heart of gold*, *heart of stone*, *a kind heart*, a *good heart*, *heartless*, and *a cold heart* to demonstrate this. However, tell them the in ancient Greece and Egypt, the liver, not the heart, was believed to be the place where the soul lived.

Instruct your students that they have to work in groups and think of their native language and how the body ties in to how the language is used. Which organs are used to show a person's personality? What do the different body organs mean metaphorically in their language? Give them ten minutes to discuss, then take feedback from students who are willing to speak.

BOOK GENRES—FANTASY ROLE-PLAY

LEVEL: *A2 (pre-intermediate) and up.*

AIMS: *Students will learn about book genres, while reviewing vocabulary related to characters in their books. Students will collaborate and work in teams to write a story and cooperate to perform it.*

RESOURCES: *This lesson plan requires a fair bit of materials, but fret not. Our aim is to procure the materials once, put them in a box, and then reuse them every time you need to perform this lesson again.*

YOU NEED A box of materials that the students are going to use to produce costumes so they can perform a short story they wrote together. I recommend loads of paper, a pair of kids' scissors, some glue, some rubber bands, some tape, and a whole host of props. I procured the ones I use from the school's lost and found. These included an umbrella, a pair of sunglasses, and a sparkly black cape. Just instruct your students that when they're done with anything from the box, they need to return it.

Introduce the students to the topic of literature. You can even briefly ask them about their favorite books if the class feels talkative enough and interested enough in books.

Elicit the term *genres*, drill pronunciation, and elicit its meaning.

A possible alternative to hangman, if you are tired of using this activity, is to instead write down the word on the board, but with the order of the words completely mixed up—R E G S N E—for example. Then, ask the students to identify the correct word.

When this is clear, divide students into groups of four, and tell them to get a piece of paper and write down a list of all the book genres they know. Assign a time limit of five minutes. Feel free to help out the class during this time as you go around and check their work.

When the time is up, explain to your students that you are looking for three genres in particular which you are hoping they will guess.

Start taking feedback from the groups, telling them if they guess the genres you are looking for. Use questions at this point to elicit more terms from your students. For example, if your students say biography, ask them, "What if I write a biography about myself, what's that called?" (Autobiography)

If students successfully guess any of the genres intended for this lesson, write them on the board. These intended genres are literary fiction, fantasy, and science fiction. After these three terms have been established, give your students two minutes in their group to discuss the differences between fantasy, literary fiction, and science fiction.

Elicit some feedback, then set up some questions as follows: "Is [fantasy/sci-fi/literary fiction] a story?" "Is the story true?" or "What is the story about?" You should get answers that tell you that all three genres contain made-up stories, but in each case the story is about different subjects. In fantasy, the story is about magical people and creatures; in science fiction, the story is about robots, new technologies, space and time travel; and in literary fiction, the story is about regular people like us.

Still in their groups, have students come up with a list of characters we find in fantasy books and a list of characters we find in science fiction books (they shouldn't go for a specific character, but rather the type of character). That is, "wizard" is correct; "Harry Potter" is not correct. Give them five minutes for this; you may walk around and check their work as you go.

When they are done, play the following guessing game: One student from one of the groups comes to your desk with their list, you choose and mark any one character that you wish, and the student has to draw it on the board. The rest of the groups have to try to guess the character. When they guess correctly, instruct the student to write the name of the character underneath it (encourage peer-correction if the students make any mistakes). Keep this exercise going as long as there are students excited to draw, but try not to let it go longer than 20 minutes.

When the game is over, instruct the students that in their group they now have to write a short story. Explain to them that for now it doesn't need to have an ending, that the story should have four characters (the same as the number of members in the team), and that the characters need to be from science fiction, from fantasy, or both. When giving such complex instructions, it's important to ask instruction-checking questions to make sure that the students have understood what they have to do. Questions you would need to ask in this case are "What do you have to do?" "Are you working alone?" "Will your story have an ending?" "How many characters are you going to come up with?" and "What kind of characters are you going to come up with?"

After about 15 minutes, explain to the students that they will be performing the story they are conjuring. Each student will take on the role of one character. Explain to the students that they will need to direct and prepare the short performance, and that they need to make costumes. Show them the box of materials, telling them that everything that gets taken out of the box needs to return at the end. Help the students out as they prepare the costumes, and help them to direct it (asking them questions like "How does a troll move, speak, stand?" etc.) Let this part take as much time as seems is necessary, up to 30 minutes. When preparations are done, ask students to perform. Give encouragement whenever you can. Some students have never even opened their mouths in a classroom; this experience might make them feel nervous.

If you have already done **Improv Storytelling** and **Mask Work**, they may be combined into this lesson for the performance.

STORYTELLING

LEVEL: *A2 (pre-intermediate) and up.*

AIMS: *Students will be exposed to a topic that they have to build a story around, so this lesson can be used to teach a variety of topics, like culture, environmental responsibility, geography, or anything that is directly related to the course. Students will engage with the themes and craft a story using the topic involved, activating their imagination and teamwork skills.*

RESOURCES: *With regard to this lesson plan, you can use as many materials as you want or have access to.*

YOU NEED TO present the theme or story that is central to the lesson; whether you recount it orally or use some resources to help you out is up to you. Students will need to present the story in their teams, and what medium they use is up to you and the resources at your disposal.

OPTIONS CAN INCLUDE actual scenes made up of the students them-selves (like short sketches or simply poses), drawings, comics, or posters depicting scenes in the story. My favorite way to do this lesson is with Legos or other plastic brick blocks. Groups are given the blocks, and they use them to build scenes in the story. Then the groups use the StoryVisualizer app on a tablet computer to capture the scenes to present them later from the app. Of course, this requires that the groups be provided with tablets and plastic brick blocks, which are not available at every school. However, the sky is the limit here; any medium you think the students can use is probably okay.

This lesson is malleable and can be adapted to the topic at hand. I use this lesson plan to teach about overtourism and Malta, as it can tie in to a cultural lesson about Malta or a lesson about ecotourism or sustainable tourism.

I present a question on the board: "Why has Malta been chosen for conducting a study about tourism and sustainability?" I pre-teach *sustainability* (in small groups, I assign the students to prepare a definition of sustainability). I ask for some answers from the classroom (this happened to be a course about overtourism and Malta, hence the very specific question. You will need to pick a relevant topic for your lesson).

I then present articles to the groups, taken from a newspaper, about the overtourism issue. After going through any difficult vocabulary, I explain to the students that in their groups, they are to put on a story linked to the overtourism issue and perform it in at least three scenes. Anything goes really—it can be a story about the effects of overtourism, about the causes, about what a particular family goes through in the circumstance, or about some legend or story which has a relevant message.

I give the students adequate time to prepare, more than 30 minutes, and then time to perform. I ask for feedback or questions about anything that wasn't clear.

This type of storytelling activity can also be done as part of a culture-themed lesson, where each group can present an element of their culture in the form of a story.

If you have a topic or theme in mind, this lesson can be applied with some creativity. I applied this process once when teaching about misrepresentation and misinformation in promotional material. I asked my students to watch the animated video "The Scarecrow" by Moonbot Studios and Chipotle on YouTube (https://www.youtube.com/watch?v=DY-GgzZKxUQ). After they did, I took feedback, asking them for their thoughts, but giving no opinion on my end, just listening to what they had to say.

Afterwards, I asked my students to watch "Honest Scarecrow" by Funny or Die at https://www.webbyawards.com/winners/2014/online-film-video/general-film-categories/video-remixes-mashups/honest-scarecrow.

When my students had watched it and understood the message, I asked them, "What was the message of the video?" After they gave me feedback, I gave each group of three students some blank paper and some writing and drawing materials and asked them to draw up a story made up of three scenes, based on the theme of the lesson.

This lesson can be applied after presenting your students with some form of material. You can show your students an article, or a photo, or you can tell them an anecdote (or half a story). Afterwards, you can ask them to create a story, in as many scenes as you wish and in whatever medium you choose, based on the theme, article, photo, or story.

USING OUR VOICES

LEVEL: *A2 (pre-intermediate) and up.*

AIMS: *Students are engaged, and humor and fun are introduced into the classroom. Students will learn how to recognize if their voice is being adequately supported by breath, which can translate to clearer, louder speech and better singing.*

RESOURCES: *None, and if you decide to follow up the explanation with a chance for the students to sing together, you can ask your students to find the lyrics on their phones.*

This lesson requires you to have some knowledge about the voice, which is aimed at showing the students correct *breath support* for singing and speaking. If this lesson is too difficult for you to understand, or things like *support* mean nothing to you, then it might be wise to skip this.

Write some names or words on the board and then ask the students to make the relevant noise or sound for what you've just written. Write down animal names so that they can make the relevant animal noise; and if you think the students can handle it, write down accents or specific famous people. After the students are sufficiently warmed up and more relaxed, write the name of a fizzy drink. You can use an actual bottle for this portion.

Ask the students to make the sound they would hear if you were opening a bottle containing a fizzy drink—the hissing sound that it makes. Have them stand up, and hold a bottle in your hand. Tell them that they are to hiss when you open the bottle and stop when you close it. Keep this up until the students have relaxed into it, even testing out how long the students can hold the hissing sound.

Ask the students to put their hand on their stomach area, and to notice any sensations that they feel underneath their hand, as they do the hissing sound again. Then ask them for feedback. The answer you expect to get is that they felt a pressing, tensing sensation in the abdomen area as they hissed out. The next time, ask the students to put their hand on their throat, and repeat the hissing exercise while noticing any sensations around the throat area. Take feedback, expecting that the throat felt relaxed, with perhaps some vibrations during the exhale, but no tensing or pushing sensations.

If the students are not quite getting to the answer that you expect, you might direct them to a different exercise, like making the owl sound, *hoot*. Instruct them to push their lips far out and make a powerful hooting sound in *head voice* (if you can, feel free to demonstrate). Ask them again to check the sensations in their stomach and their throat as they make the hooting sound.

If they are still not getting it, ensure that they are making a loud hooting sound (that is, they are not trying to keep it soft) and that they are pushing out their lips (I usually tell them that their lips need to be pushed out like they're about to kiss someone).

After they do this correctly, you might demonstrate the observations on the board, on a drawing of a human torso, which demonstrates how our abdomen should feel pressure but our throat should feel relaxed when we are using our voice. Explain that this is called *breath support* and that using the right breath support helps us not get tired if we have to speak for a long time and project our voice; and it protects our voice if we are singing.

If your students are struggling to feel the engagement in their abdomen, check that they are standing up straight.

If they still can't get it, ask them to imagine they are in a library and they want to indicate to someone to keep quiet. Ask them to show you how they would do it, putting a finger to their lips and hushing someone softly. Ask them to do it again, but take a breath in first, and trying to make the hush last as long as they can. As they do this, they should feel the engagement in their abdomen. Ask them to put their hand on their stomach while they do the hush.

When everyone is caught up, I allow for some singing fun in class. I let my students pick a song that the entire class can sing together that is in English (and if the students are young, I ask that the song chosen does not include any crude lyrics or swear words). I let the students google the lyrics on their phone if they need it, and we proceed to sing (with correct breath support).

HOW DO I MAKE THAT?

LEVEL: *A1 (beginner) and up.*

AIMS: *Students will discuss the fun topic of cooking. Students will learn cooking terms like frying and then write up a recipe.*

RESOURCES: *For lower levels, pictures of cooking terms (see the examples at the end of this lesson)*

When working with very low levels (A1) for this lesson, I like to make use of visuals to explain cooking terms (at the end of the lesson). Just take this book with you to class, and show the pictures.

Open the topic of food in any way you like. A few options could be writing down a question or two on the board, asking students to discuss them in pairs, and then getting feedback. Some questions could be "What is your favorite food?" "How often do you eat out?" or "Do you eat food from different countries when you travel?"

Play hangman with the word *recipe* and ask the students how to pronounce it. If none of them gets it, it's important to drill it at this point. Ask your students what a recipe is. Scaffold and help them get it if they can't. Explain that we find recipes in specific books and online.

Take this moment to teach all the important cooking terms in English. Use the photos on the next page, showing them one by one, and ask students what is happening and what they see in each picture. It's likely that your students will describe the food, for example, *egg*. However, direct your students and scaffold so they can tell you how the food is being cooked.

Don't just give them a term, such as *fry*, and stop there, but rather get them to explain what *fry* means, that is, cooking something in hot oil (in a pan). *Boil* means heating water. (A student once put his hand up and explained that the water had to be at 100 degrees Celsius). Use gestures, if needed, to explain what slicing is.

Note that when I say *scaffold*, what that means is that you do not give the answer away to students, but rather help them build it up. Make sure they've understood, before you give away the answer. If, for example, you are asking the students about picture 4, let them show you, even mime, the stirring motion with their fingers, so that you can see that they are understanding what's going on. Then, you can give away the answer, *stir*.

Tell your students that together, you are going to write the recipe for how to make a cup of English tea on the board. Scaffold and work with them slowly, especially if they are low-level, and guide them toward the answer:

1. Boil water in a kettle.
2. Put a teabag into a mug (and sugar or honey).
3. Pour hot water into mug.
4. Wait for five minutes.
5. Stir the hot water, and remove the teabag.
6. Add milk and stir.

Have students form groups of three. Explain the task: Working together, they have 15 minutes to write down a recipe for any dish they choose. Concept-check to make sure they understood the instructions. (What do you have to do? What do you have to write? Are you working alone?)

If you notice your students choosing to rely on google Translate, let them, as long as it's a word or two, not the whole thing, provided this does not go against your school's rules.

If they are low-level students, they will choose simpler recipes—like pasta with tomato sauce, or toast, or a smoothie—which is perfectly fine. If they are high-level students, feel free to challenge them to come up with something a bit more complex.

When the exercise is complete, you can ask a representative from each group to write their recipe on the board one by one, perform error correction together, and drill the pronunciation of any difficult words.

Extra activity: How do you like your ___?

Now that your students have learned so many cooking terms, you can ask them variations of the above question, such as "How do you like your chicken [or eggs, fish, potatoes, etc.]?" and get answers like "fried," "boiled," "grilled," "baked," "sliced." You can let them answer these questions in their groups, and then get feedback.

»   *Photocopy the images on pages 47-49 or download full-color worksheets at http://www.alphabetpublishingbooks.com/book/instant-efl-lesson-plans.*

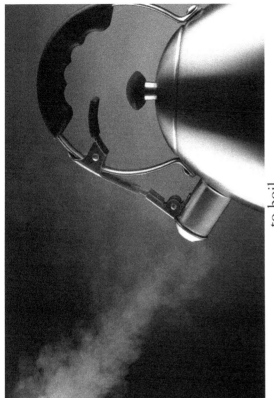

to boil

to dice

to bake

to mix

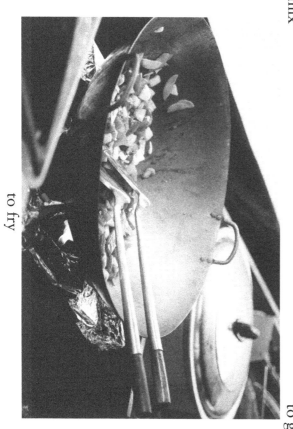

to fry

to grill

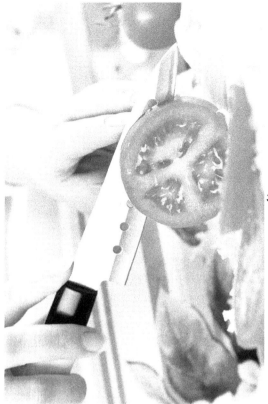

to slice

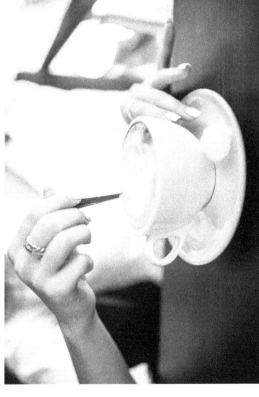

to stir

to roast

MEMES

LEVEL: *B2 (upper intermediate) and up.*

AIMS: *Humor is inspired in the classroom. Students will explain or better acquaint themselves with the online world of memes. Students will work in teams and put their creativity to use. Students will see differences in humor and how a joke can be hard to understand for a learner of English, as opposed to a native speaker.*

RESOURCES: *Your students need an internet connection on their phones. You can show your students a couple of memes. You can print and laminate a couple of memes, or just show the memes on your phone.*

Elicit the term *memes*. Ask your students to explain to you what memes are. Students will come up with many wonderful definitions. The one I would be looking for is "a picture with a funny caption," and I help my students produce a similar definition. If none of the students know what a meme is, invite them to find "Classical Art Memes" on Facebook on their phones and look at it, and then ask them what they think it means. At this point, show your students the first meme that you've prepared, and notice their reaction. Ask any students that laughed if they can explain the meme, and what was funny about it. To the students that did not laugh, you can ask them why they didn't like the meme.

Repeat the process with the second meme, if you have it. Point out to the students that some are laughing and some are not, and ask why that is. Get the students to explain to you that jokes or memes won't be universally funny. Get them to explain or see that some jokes are not understandable across cultures. Others will only be understandable to a native English speaker, because the joke might be based on a word or phrase having more than one meaning, like wordplay.

Show your students Cartoon 1 at the end of this lesson (or present them with photocopies of the picture). Tell them that it's a meme, but is lacking the caption.Ask your students to work in pairs (or alone – depending on how many students there are). Tell them to come up with a caption to make a funny meme, giving a time limit of 2 to 5 minutes.

When students are done, get them to show their memes with the captions. Discuss the reactions to the memes, at this point. See which jokes worked, which didn't work, which needed to be explained, and what other barriers there were to the joke being understood. You can take the meme which was the most successful and attach it to the board, if you have the means.

Present Cartoon 2 to the students as photocopies and cutouts, and assign the students into groups (or let them form groups as they go). Tell them to pick a picture in their group, and that they have 10 minutes to turn this picture into a meme. They can add on (as in draw) more things onto these pictures, and most importantly, come up with a funny caption. At the, end, assign adequate time to go over each meme.

Give your students 30 minutes (but let the activity run longer if it needs to) and tell them that they are to work on making their own digital memes. Give them some scratch paper to draft on (if you have scratch paper available), before they make their final versions in digital format using their phones and an internet connection. There are many meme generating websites online that they can get creative with, one of the simpler ones being https://imgflip.com/memegenerator. Let them cooperate with each other if they want. You should not need to direct very much; it's possible your students will know more about memes and creating them than you do.

When the students are done, get them to show their memes to the rest of the class. It's interesting to discuss the same points again here. Which memes were found funny by everyone, which memes were only funny to a small part of the classroom, and other such observations can be discussed.

If any memes were very popular, you can have them printed and hung up somewhere in the classroom.

Caption 1

Caption 2

IMPROV STORYTELLING

LEVEL: *B1 (intermediate) and up.*

AIMS: *Students will approach some of their fears. Students will be shown what improv is and how fun it can be. Students will develop their imagination or performing skills and build their confidence in these abilities.*

RESOURCES: *Just some role cards (found at the end of this lesson), which you only need to print once, and can then reuse every time you want to carry out this lesson again.*

THIS IS ONE of my favorite lesson plans. I tend to automatically go for this one when I'm asked to replace a teacher and have a class for only one session. It is not what the students are expecting, and there is a next-to-zero chance that they've already done the same lesson with the other teacher.

Try to establish a warm and friendly atmosphere in the classroom. If they are your regular students, feel free to start off by asking them how their day or weekend or whatever has been, or to tell them about your own. If they are new students, find out all their names and get them to share a little bit about themselves, asking for more information. As much as you can, you would like the students to feel safe in this class.

Ask for a volunteer. However, I prefer going for a student who is a little bit shy for this lesson. When a student puts their hand up and you can tell that this is one of the more confident and self-assured students in the group, ask that student instead to help you find someone who is a bit shy.

Once you have your volunteer, invite the volunteer to the center of the classroom, and ask them to tell you a story. Give the following specific instructions: "I want you to invent and tell us a story." The reactions you get to this are always unique and I usually prefer to note them. If they ask for further clarification, explain that the story can be about anything they want, and it must be made up on the spot, not real. You will find that some students will be able to do this task, perhaps even for several minutes. Others will not be able to accomplish it. Many will feel uncomfortable. If they remain stuck for over a minute, invite them to return to their seat. Ask a second volunteer to perform this exercise, and a third, if you wish.

Notice how everyone reacts differently, and you can even point this out to them. Sometimes students hold themselves back because they feel their story is not interesting or original. It's important to let them know that you didn't ask for a good story, just a story. Teach them that they don't need to expect perfection. If you think they're ready for it, you can share theater director Keith Johnstone's quote, "Be more average." Let the students discuss it. You can explain that Johnstone was encouraging his students to let go of perfectionism and the need to be unique, as these hindered improv actors.

At this point, it's a good idea to switch it up. Invite another student to be the storyteller. It's okay if the student is a bit nervous, because you're going to help them. Let them stand in the center, and instruct all the other students that they have 15 seconds to think of a word (or a noun, or an adjective, as you prefer). Then, explain that you want your volunteer to start telling the story, but that, when you see that they are stuck, you are going to call out "pause" and point at a student, who will immediately say their word. The storyteller has to continue telling the story, but find some way to incorporate the word that was just said to them into the story. Check understanding by asking your storyteller what their role is and the other participants what their role is.

Let the exercise go on for a good five or even ten minutes, and whenever you want the story to take on a new direction, or when your storyteller seems to be struggling, say, "pause," and point at a student who will give the student a word to use in his story.

When this exercise has gone on long enough, then let a new story-teller be selected. I suggest somebody who is a close friend of the original storyteller, if possible. Instruct this storyteller that they must continue the story where their friend left off and that they also must reincorporate into the story all the words that were said by the participants during the first part of the story. Let the story develop into a gradual ending.

Now that the students understand the task, ask them if anybody else would like to give the exercise a try, and invite any volunteer who feels up to the task to do it. They can choose if they want helping words or not. When the exercise is complete, get some feedback from students. Ask questions like these:

- Are you good at this kind of exercise? Why?
- Would you enjoy having to do this exercise very often?
- How do you feel when you have to tell a story like this in front of everyone?
- Is it easier when you are being fed words that you have to use, or is it easier when you are completely in charge of the story?

At some point, a student is going to bring up imagination, or lack thereof. If they don't, you can bring it up and discuss it.

The class now needs to be split into two groups of equal size. On one side you should have the students who claim they don't have imagination, or that they are too shy to create a story, and on the other side you should have the students who feel somewhat comfortable with this exercise. If there is no way to split the group equally in this way, then just do a round of counting to establish each person's group. (A, B, A, B, A, B . . .)

Instruct every student A to buddy up with a student B, move their chairs to somewhere in the room where they have some distance from the other pairs, and face each other. Give each student their role card, instructing them to read it without showing it to anybody. When everyone has had time to read their instructions, let the exercise start, and set a time limit of around 15 minutes. If there's an odd number of students, the teacher can buddy up with a student, but the student should be in group B.

When the exercise is done, invite each student B, one by one, to come to the front of the classroom, and tell the story that they have extracted from student A during the exercise. After each student B completes the story, ask this student some questions such as these:

- Do you like this story?
- Do you think your partner is good at telling stories? Do they have a good imagination?

These questions will likely elicit giggles from the rest of the classroom. When the exercise is over, let all the students exchange role cards so they understand the meaning of the exercise. After all gasps of surprise have died down, you can elicit feedback from the class, asking them what they can learn from this exercise. If the answer doesn't come out explicitly, you can guide your students toward the answer that everyone has imagination: sometimes we just block it, but it is always there. If the audience is mature enough, you can explain that once the responsibility of creating, inventing, and sharing a story was taken away, everyone happily imagined the questions to ask.

A.	B.
Your partner B thinks that you are going to create a story, but they are wrong, they will be the ones creating the story without realizing.	Your partner has a story in their mind—but they are not going to tell you the story. Instead, you have to ask them yes-or-no questions to extract the story.
Partner B is going to ask you questions to understand the story. For example, "Is it about a house?" which you will have to answer.	Try to understand and learn as much as you can about the story, as later you will be sharing it with the class.
However, the rules are that if the question ends with a consonant, the answer is going to be no. If the question ends with a vowel, the answer will be yes, and if the question ends in y, the answer is maybe.	Is the story about a cat? Does it live near here? Have you ever met it?
Is the story about a fairy?—*Maybe* Is she sad?—*No* Does she live in a small house?—*Yes*	

© 2019 Cristian Spiteri from *Instant EFL Lesson Plans: 25 Creative, Highly Engaging Lesson Plans from Practically Nothing*

Mask Work

LEVEL: *A2 (pre-intermediate) and up.*

AIMS: *Students will perform in front of people, under the protection of a mask. Students can understand what an improv actor does, and students get to enjoy making masks and performing in a group. This exercise is effective for public speaking skills or for building confidence in speaking and performing in front of other people in a second language.*

RESOURCES: *Tools that the students might need to make masks, such as blank A4 paper, rubber bands, pencils, a pair of scissors.*

Ask the students to return the rubber bands and the scissors at the end of the lesson (so you can reuse this activity). The only material you will need to replenish is the paper, which I usually take from my school's photocopier. Some schools also have a hoard of scratch paper; and provided it is blank on one side, it can safely be used for this activity. Keep the tools in a box, so you will only need to replenish the supply of paper every time you do this activity. That way, this doesn't require planning or procuring any materials except for the first time.

Keith Johnstone's book *Improv: Improvisation and the Theatre* is the inspiration behind this lesson plan. I highly recommend reading it.

This lesson can stand on its own, but I also recommend merging it with other lessons if it seems appropriate. I have sometimes blended it with **At the Restaurant** and **Improv Storytelling** with great success.

You may want to spend a few minutes focusing on emotions and pre-teaching them before starting the mask work, but this is optional. When you're ready, hand out the tools and explain to the students that they may work in pairs if they wish, but their job is to make a mask that will fit their face and that they can wear. If you have previously taught emotions, you may ask the students to each pick an emotion and design a mask that depicts the emotion. If you haven't taught emotions, then tell the students that they can let themselves be inspired, or they can just start working on their mask and then see what turns up. Tell them that their final mask does not necessarily need to be human.

Let the students try on their masks, making sure they fit. If you haven't read Johnstone's book, in summary, it says that when our face is hidden, we can become much more uninhibited, which is why they help us build confidence.

However, I suggest that some rules be specified for the students before they put on their masks, to ensure a smooth lesson. I usually give the following rules, and make the students repeat them back to me:

- Speak English in class.
- Do not leave the class without permission.
- Do not hurt each other.
- Remember that our purpose is to have fun and to learn.
- When I say the magic word, everybody has to take off their mask.
- I let the students come up with the magic word.

There are many ways you can use the masks in class. If you want to use this lesson on its own, which is what I'll describe, it can be used to make the students practice improv theater. It's good for building confidence and speaking skills in a foreign language, and it's surprisingly fun.

Alternatively, this can be made to fit the lesson **At the Restaurant**—where everybody has a mask on—or it can be used as part of **Improv Storytelling**—with the masks being used for their presentation and performance of the story. The masks can also be used in **Book Genres—Fantasy Role-Play**, if needed.

Present the words *improv theater* and *improv actor* to the students and ask if anybody knows what they mean. If nobody does, guide them to the answers that improv actors perform in shows where they have no prepared script or plan. Explain to the students that they are going to be performing improv theater in groups, but if they are stuck, the rest of the class will be able to help them out. Also explain the concept of *blocking* in improv, and demonstrate an example.

Blocking is when an actor (or in this case classmate) makes a suggestion or tries to take the story in a direction and someone else shuts them down completely. An actor might say "I bet if we went to the moon, somebody there might be able to help us." If someone else says "No, we can't go to the moon" or something of the sort that shuts down the idea, that's called blocking. Tell them that blocking is not allowed during the performance. A more appropriate answer would be "How can we get to the moon then? Who can help us get there?"

Say that when they start performing, you will be the one to tell them when the performance is over. Tell them that it should take around 20 minutes, and that when five minutes are left, you will let them know.

Divide your students into groups. Have the first group to perform put on their masks, and also ask them to look at themselves in their selfie cameras, to see what they look like with the mask on. Then let the performance start. It's normal, although not too common, if your students hesitate a bit during the performance. Do not pressure them. You can prompt them to move along the story by asking questions such as "Do you notice anything strange?" "What happened next?" "Where did you go?" or "Who can help you with this?" If you notice anybody blocking, say, "No blocking," and remind the students when the performance only has five minutes left. Repeat the same process with all the groups.

You should have a magic word that reminds your students to take off their masks. Some students may go over the top when they have the mask on, which is why you want a way to tell everybody to come back to a calm state.

LEARNING A LANGUAGE FROM SCRATCH

LEVEL: *any.*

AIMS: *Students will gain linguistic skills and knowledge through the study of a completely foreign language. Students will be able to apply these skills to English.*

RESOURCES: *Whatever you deem appropriate for teaching the basics of this other language, like worksheets. I recommend preparing or procuring the worksheets once, and then reusing them whenever necessary.*

Before taking the initiative to teach another language in class, I recommend speaking to the director and getting their approval. If the course is culturally-themed, this lesson would be appropriate. In addition, it makes for a change of pace, and learning the new language could be interesting in showing them links to English or to their own language. Furthermore, it reminds students of their skills to communicate non-verbally, and with limited vocabulary, but relying on gestures and other cues.

I regularly teach cultural courses in Malta, so I opt to teach a basic lesson in the Maltese language on the final day, as it's quite easy and a nice break.

Maltese is naturally a very readable language (meaning it is spoken very closely to the way it is written)—so I teach my students the Maltese alphabet, drilling it and then I test them. I may ask them what they notice in common with other languages they know. After this, I hand out some worksheets where students can work out the numbers and some basic phrases in Maltese, and then I have them say them to me, and I test them with the numbers.

When they are done and able to read some basic phrases, then I ask them to work in pairs, and I have them think of a phrase they wish to say to their partner. I instruct them to type it into google Translate and have them say it in Maltese to their partner.

SOLO-TRAVEL

LEVEL: *B1 (intermediate) and up.*

AIMS: *Students will do their own research about a particular destination, learning about maps and attractions in the process. Students will plan a solo-trip, which can be empowering.*

RESOURCES: *I usually recommend students use their phones or laptops for research, but I don't really use any resources. Worksheets are an option, if you wish to pre-teach some travel lexis.*

USE ANY METHOD you prefer for introducing the topic of travel or doing any pre-teaching. I like to pre-teach vocabulary like *hostels* and *hotels*, *accommodation*, *street food*, *itinerary*, *trips*, *luxurious*, *budget*, *tourist attractions*, and *tourist traps*.

Ask your students about traveling solo. Have they ever done it? Would they do it? Do they think it's scary? Why? Any interesting stories?

Put a list of websites on the board that are all related to travel, in random positions. Examples include Kiwi, Expedia, google Flights, Hostelworld, Couchsurfing, Wikitravel, AirfareWatchdog, TripAdvisor, google Maps, Momondo, Luxury Retreats. Assign your students some time (ten to fifteen minutes) to take a look at these websites (probably from their phone) and then tell you what these websites are for. Ask for more information if the answers are vague or not detailed enough. For instance, if your students say that both Hostelworld and Luxury Retreats are used to find accommodation, you can ask them then if both of those websites are the same and give you the same result. The answer is obviously that one is more luxurious and expensive than the other.

Explain to your students what you want from them: They are to plan a solo-trip to a destination they've never been to but would like to go to. They have to pick the dates and then decide on the accommodation, the activities, and even the restaurants if they want—a thorough itinerary. Explain that the trip must be realistic and make logistical sense if viewed on a map. Ask them if they're going to rent a car. Instruct them that if their trip is very long, like a month in India, then they do not need to prepare an itinerary for the whole month; three or four days should be fine.

Give students the appropriate time to prepare the itinerary, up to an hour. At the end, have them all present their itineraries, showing photos and explaining their trips and why they made the decisions they did. You can even have students vote for their favorite itinerary, saying why.

INSTANT GAMES

BACK TO THE BOARD

THIS IS A life-saver when you have ten more minutes in a lesson, but your lesson material is over, you want a game that can help the lesson come to a close, and you're bored with hangman.

Ask for a volunteer, and place this volunteer in front of the white-board, on a seat, facing toward the class. Instruct the volunteer that they are not to look at the whiteboard. Explain that you are going to write the name of a famous person on the whiteboard. The volunteer's role is to figure out who that famous person is, and they can help themselves by asking yes-or-no questions to the classroom. When they have guessed, they can pick another participant who will take the seat in front of the board. You can keep writing names yourself, or you can ask the students to write the names if you've run out of ideas or want to involve your students more.

Here are some suggestions of names:

Anybody from the Harry Potter universe, such as Draco Malfoy	Famous politicians or first wives/husbands, such as Michelle Obama
Classical names like Shakespeare or Dickens	Mr. Bean
Famous singers or pop icons like Beyoncé	Anybody from The Simpsons' universe, such as Homer
Stephen Hawking	Elon Musk
Famous athletes	Marilyn Monroe

BLACK MAGIC

THIS IS A famous party game. Explain the rules of black magic to one student, perhaps during a break or before lesson. Then play it with the one chosen student, and allow the students to make any suggestions or try to figure out the rules.

Rules of black magic: Two participants (agreed on beforehand) will claim to have a telepathic connection. When the first participant is out of earshot, the class will indicate a mystery object in the room to the second participant. The first participant is at this point invited in, and the second participant indicates object after object in the room, asking if it is the mystery object that the class had indicated. The first participant should respond yes or no appropriately when asked if each object is the mystery object. It will go something like:

"Is it the marker?"
"No"
"Is it the board?"
"No"
"Is it the pair of trousers?"
"Yes"

The secret of the game, which the class has to figure out, is that the second participant will only indicate the correct object after they have previously indicated a black object. So, in the example above, it would mean that the board was black; hence, trousers was the correct answer.

Initiate a discussion where students try to guess how the game works. Let them know if they got it right, or you can give away the secret at the end.

There are other explanations and variations of this rule and this game available online, if you need any.

HANGMAN

THIS IS THE most basic EFL and classroom game since time immemorial.

The teacher (or participant) has to prepare a word or a phrase in their mind. Then, they step up to the board, and write down the word, but instead of letters, they just write blank lines. So if the phrase is ice-cream, they write _ _ _ _ _ _ _ _.

The classroom's objective is to guess the word. They do this by raising their hand, and when the teacher points at them, they offer a letter.

If the letter is present in the word, then the teacher will write down the letter in the appropriate space. If the letter is not present in the word, then the teacher draws a component of the diagram of a hanged man.

This process is repeated, until either the word is complete or the drawing of the hanged man is complete. The students win if they successfully guess the word. If they fail and the hanged man drawing is completed, then they lose.

BONUS CHAPTER

As a token of appreciation for having purchased the book and gotten this far into it, I've prepared some bonus content that I would like to share with you. A link is included underneath, and clicking it (or copying it into your web browser) will allow you to sign up for my newsletter. You will immediately receive the bonus chapter, "Instant Teacher Training Course from Practically Nothing". In addition, you'll be on my newsletter list, and I'll be able to send you more materials that are valuable for your career as a teacher.

The bonus material builds on the content in the main book, and keeps in line with getting you to work without requiring stressful levels of preparation.

Unfortunately teachers are not (always) adequately paid for the hours they spend in preparation, and I've always believed that teachers deserve some quality, effective resources that they can put to work easily, and the right to enjoy their free time and lunch breaks in peace.

https://mailchi.mp/346e5a940bcc/instanteflbonus

ABOUT THE AUTHOR

CRISTIAN SPITERI has been a language teacher for seven years, working with students from all over the world. This is his first book. He's always known he wanted to be an author, and has been featured in several publications on Medium, writing mainly about LGBTQ issues, travel, self-awareness, and mental health.

When not writing or teaching, Cris is usually busy globetrotting, acting, recording voice-overs and music in his studio, or catching some of West End's latest and best shows. All his different pursuits have definitely had their mark on his teaching style, as you can tell from the diverse activities in this book.